CONTENTS

ANOREXIA NERVOSA

Guidelines for

Assessment and Treatment

in

Arrowe Park Hospita

Nursing & ~~Midwifery Libr~~

2nd Edition

by

A H Crisp and Lisa McClelland

Based on "The St George's Approach",
developed by Professor Crisp and his teams
at the Middlesex and St George's Hospital Medical Schools,
over the period 1960-1994.

Psychology Press
An imprint of Erlbaum (UK) Taylor & Francis

Copyright © 1996 by Psychology Press
an imprint of Erlbaum (UK) Taylor & Francis Ltd.

1st Edition © 1994 by A H Crisp and Lisa McClelland,
Department of Mental Health Sciences,
St George's Hospital Medical School

Psychology Press
27 Church Road
Hove
East Sussex, BN3 2FA
UK

British Library Cataloguing in Publication Data

A catalogue record for this book is available from the British Library

ISBN 0-86377-409-1

Typeset by HH Design
Printed in Great Britain by Redwood Books, Trowbridge, Wiltshire

ACKNOWLEDGEMENTS

The line drawings were done by a male patient whilst undergoing treatment 20 years ago and are reproduced again in this book with our gratitude.

Figure 1 (page 4) is reproduced by permission of the Editor, *British Medical Journal*, from Crisp A H (1983) Anorexia nervosa (Regular review) *British Medical Journal* **287** 855-858.

Figure 2 (page 10) and the Table on page 15 are reproduced by permission of the editors from Crisp, A H (1991) The anorectic woman: abnormal body experience and adolescence. In: *Advanced Psychosomatic Research in Obstetrics and Gynecology*, Springer-Verlag, Berlin; 145-153.

PREFACE

The majority of general practitioners and other district medical and psychiatric services will not have immediate access to a specialist treatment service for anorexia nervosa but will encounter these patients who are very difficult to help and be required to provide treatment.

This booklet is a guide for non-specialist clinicians dealing with these patients. Within it are basic and general guidelines on their care drawn from our views concerning the nature of the condition.

The proposal, of an initial thorough assessment, followed by a dozen or so skilled and supervised psychotherapy interventions by the same person or in close co-operation with that person, coupled with expert dietary help, and leading to time-limited but meaningful support for a considerable time thereafter, is not presented as the ideal. It is presented as a realistic, minimum necessary effective intervention that can help significantly in a proportion of cases, and lay the foundations for more substantial help in many other instances.

I. INTRODUCTION

Anorexia nervosa creates endless suffering for individuals and their families. It is important, therefore, to try to identify cases early and then to intervene with an effective treatment to reduce mortality and the severe physical, psychological and social handicaps that stem from the chronic condition.

It is not a rare disorder. Estimated prevalence figures range from around 0.03% to sometimes as much as 8% in certain high risk groups such as ballet dancers and dieticians (when those prone to the condition and attracted to such activities have not been screened out at the point of recruitment). It is somewhat more often found in the higher social classes and is predominantly a female disorder (males make up about 3 or 4 % of all cases). The average age of onset is in the late teens, but cases of early premenarchal onset (as young as 9 or 10 years) and late onset (older than 25 years) occur.

Anorexia nervosa can run in families and there is evidence of a genetic component. Family characteristics have been described: e.g. alcohol dependence in one parent, undue preoccupation with feeding, physical fitness and other attempts at extreme mastery of the body, a propensity to respond to life stresses with avoidance or depression. Brüch (1978) felt that family members functioned as if they could read each others' minds; Minuchin (1978) described them as being enmeshed, conflict avoidant, rigid, overprotective and involving the patient in the unresolved parental conflicts. Crisp (1967, 1980) has suggested that the essence of the condition is the **phobic avoidance** of **normal** body weight in those predisposed to such defensive strategies, which then crystallises out as a persistent adaptation to the strains that adolescence brings to such family relationships.

Recently, attempts have been made to standardise the diagnosis both here in the UK and in North America. (See Appendix 1 for DSM-IV and ICD 10 criteria).

Anorexia nervosa can be a silent disorder and often goes unnoticed in the early stages, thereby allowing it to become well established and difficult to treat. Long term follow-up studies which have examined the natural history of the disorder paint a dismal picture. After 20 years 12-20% of patients have died — half by suicide (Ratnasurya, 1991, Theander, 1985). However, 30% have made a good recovery in terms of weight, food control, psychological and social function, and 20-30% show an intermediate recovery; whilst the remaining 20-30% have a very poor lifelong outcome in all aspects of their existence.

Appropriate treatment can be effective. In the short term it can lead to a sustained increase in weight and an improvement in psycho-social functioning. Long term benefits have been demonstrated by a marked reduction in mortality (Crisp et al. 1992).

The first step in helping a person with anorexia nervosa is to generate a formulation based on the assessment of the patient, the family and a knowledge of the **psychopathology**, which can then inform and shape the treatment. **The assessment interview is crucial in this respect.** It also serves to engage the individual and the family in becoming 'patients' who want to be actively involved in treatment. Thus, we define 'patients' as people who have decided they have a condition which they would rather not have and hope there is someone around who may be able to help them get rid of it.

When the same point is made more than once in the following text this is deliberate and is intended to indicate its key role in this approach to the condition.

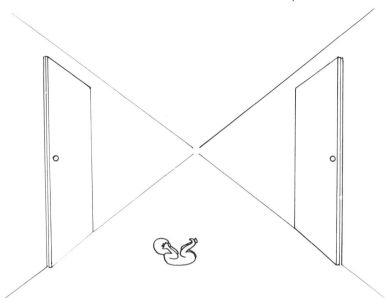

THE NATURE OF THE PSYCHOPATHOLOGY

The clinical approach set out in this book rests on our view of the psychopathology driving the condition (see Crisp 1967, 1980). The disorder is seen as pivoting psycho-dynamically around the experience of puberty and its unavoidable prompting of the tasks of adolescence. Such challenging tasks begin to confront us within the second decade of our lives and require adequate resolution if pathological reaction is not to arise. Occasionally they can be resurrected later in life when earlier insubstantial and brittle adjustments break down, e.g. when new conflictual intimate relationships develop, childbirth occurs, parents die, the menopause/involution supervenes. Late onset cases of anorexia nervosa under these circumstances can then occur but are rare.

A variety of family relationships and childhood influences can render individuals particularly vulnerable to the experience of puberty. Such development may then be experienced as alien, threatening, as getting beyond control (e.g. the impact of sexuality on the self or the family), or dangerous because of inevitable

Figure 1. TYPICAL EVOLUTION OF ANOREXIA NERVOSA

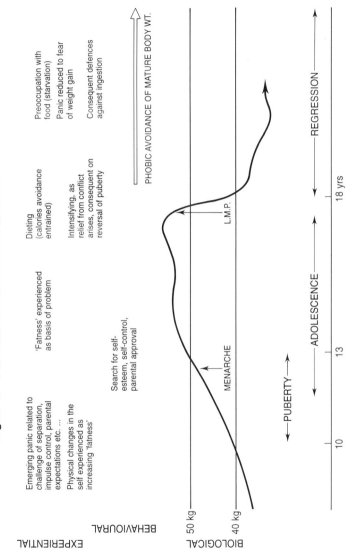

Emerging panic related to challenge of separation, impulse control, parental expectations etc. ....

Physical changes in the self experienced as increasing 'fatness'

'Fatness' experienced as basis of problem

Search for self-esteem, self-control, parental approval

Dieting (calories avoidance entrained)

Intensifying, as relief from conflict arises, consequent on reversal of puberty

Preoccupation with food (starvation)

Panic reduced to fear of weight gain

Consequent defences against ingestion

PHOBIC AVOIDANCE OF MATURE BODY WT.

EXPERIENTIAL

BEHAVIOURAL

BIOLOGICAL

50 kg

40 kg

MENARCHE

L.M.P.

←—PUBERTY—→

←—ADOLESCENCE—→

←—REGRESSION—→

10

13

18 yrs

4

separation from parents, etc. In anorexia nervosa such insecurity/panic/shame becomes attributed to the development of body shape and its basis, in the female, of normal 'fatness'. This 'fatness' with its post-pubertal sexual basis can then come to be experienced as 'not owned' and alien, a dangerous and unwanted identity challenge. Efforts to control and regulate it escalate. The suddenness with which calorie restraint then takes over reflects the profound relief experienced from the reversal of the pubertal process itself. Once puberty is banished, problems it had prompted are resolved. Thereafter the individual rapidly develops a phobia of any weight gain above about 7 stones (44.5 kg) in the female (varying slightly with height) or about 8 stones (50.8 kg) in the male (again varying with height).

This avoidance mechanism (see Figure 1) will usually be denied vigorously. The back-to-the-wall/ refuge/ unfulfilling aspects of the condition will also often be denied. The anorectic literally has nowhere else to hide and, if necessary, death by suicide may be preferred. The loss of any sense of self, the subordination of all feelings to the fear of weight gain and the inability to differentiate them, all of which are an inevitable product of the disorder itself, now massively block communication with others. Panic about weight gain drives the anorectic.

The family becomes locked into a secondary battle over feeding. This is non-specific, largely unrelated to the prior developmental problem (now resolved, and possibly never shared) that originally precipitated out the disorder. It is a serious error to judge this current conflict about feeding as primary to the disorder, though it can reveal the personalities involved and the relevance of the condition to all concerned.

In summary, the psychopathology of anorexia nervosa pivots around the meaning of normal body weight and shape. It is an avoidance stance in relation to this pathology. It is not primarily an eating disorder in psychopathological terms. It is a panic disorder with adult weight, and any movement towards it, being the feared object. It is quite unrelated to the feeding disorders of childhood. It bears some relationship to bulimia nervosa, but the latter exists at normal adult body weight levels and the biologically based avoidance mechanism which is the hallmark of anorexia nervosa, and which drives its natural history, has not been harnessed. Anorexia nervosa rarely occurs in the male but when it does (Crisp, 1995), similar mechanisms are at work i.e. the disorder is also reduced to the final common pathway of energy (calories) being withdrawn from the developmental process which is then selectively aborted.

Differential diagnosis

This can be one of the most complex in the medical field.

Psychiatric:

The disorder can often be misperceived as being primarily a depressive or obsessive/compulsive disorder rather than that the former is a reaction to the failed adjustment and the latter a personality-related defence buttressing avoidance of weight gain in the condition. The panic features themselves may be concealed, or may express themselves without apparent reference to their real origins of weight concern. Agoraphobic and anxious social behaviour may be very evident and in fact rooted in such fears as loss of the ability to control eating except in very personal and secretive circumstances. Substance abuse including alcohol abuse can become a chronic feature. Psychosis may even be suspected in view of the bizarre ideation and over-valued ideas. When psychosis does coexist, which is rarely, then the content is rooted in 'anorectic' thinking e.g. food is *believed* to be 'poisonous' or 'alive'. A variety of DSM-IV Axis 2 diagnoses (personality disorder) can be identified but it is difficult to interpret these as the presentation is coloured by state effects and starvation effects.

Organic:

On the physical side, anorexia nervosa is both one of the easiest and most difficult disorders to diagnose. As indicated above it has a specific psychopathology which in our view is necessary to establish the diagnosis. It is the second level of diagnosis (see below) that is pathognomonic of the syndrome. If the clear diagnosis is proving difficult to make one must consider the range of possible 'physical' explanations. On the one hand the impasse may reflect continued successful denial of the psychopathology by the patient. On the other hand, obviously, there can be other causes for the weight loss. Thus, clearly there are many organic conditions that can also present with such weight loss though the commonest cause of substantial weight loss in adolescent females in the developed world is undoubtedly anorexia nervosa.

It is usually possible to make a very positive diagnosis of anorexia nervosa, if it is present. However, any patient presenting with atypical features should be reassessed regularly to exclude other occult organic pathology. More commonly, however, anorectic patients offer a seemingly plausible physical explanation for their weight loss. Family members who are searching for a physical explanation to their child's weight loss, collude with this denial e.g. "I don't know why she has lost weight, she eats all her meals with us." Both patient and parents can hold this belief with conviction even in the face of clear and marked weight loss. Overall, anorectics have been found to report their food intake as being double its actual amount. Clues to denial can be found in the patient's response to discussion of body shape and size in terms of acceptable weight, maximum tolerated weights and ideal weight. Denial can be exposed by prescribing a diet predicting the appropriate weight gain and monitoring this with the patient. When denial is firmly entrenched the weight phobia can only be exposed in an in-patient setting, where the patient cannot flee the dietary regime or take compensatory action after eating.

Such complex differential diagnostic problems are discussed in detail elsewhere (Crisp 1977).

★   ★   ★

In the following sections of the book, reference to 'her' often also means 'him', although from time to time both terms are included.

II. APPROACH TO THE ASSESSMENT

The whole family should be required to attend the first interview which, as we have already indicated, also has the potential to be a first therapeutic intervention. There are advantages in meeting with the parents first, taking a systematic history of the illness from them and then histories of their own personal developments and relationships. Optimise their capacities to talk about such matters. They may have particular difficulty in talking about any infidelities and sexual abuse.

The anorectic will have concluded meanwhile that you are colluding with the parents' views of the problem. This will need to be dealt with when you meet with her.

At the end of the three hour assessment you will aim to have enabled not only her but also her parents to become 'patients'. Detailed written descriptions and video portrayals of our own assessment procedure are available (see Appendix 2).

PSYCHOPATHOLOGY

The initial diagnosis, pursued in this way, is made at 3 levels (see Figure 2):

Level 1: Behavioural

Here one is tapping the symptoms and signs of malnutrition and low body weight.

The starvation syndrome itself contributes behaviourial effects such as bingeing, hoarding and stealing food, and cognitive effects such as preoccupation with food, awareness of hunger.

Figure 2. THE THREE LEVELS OF DIAGNOSIS

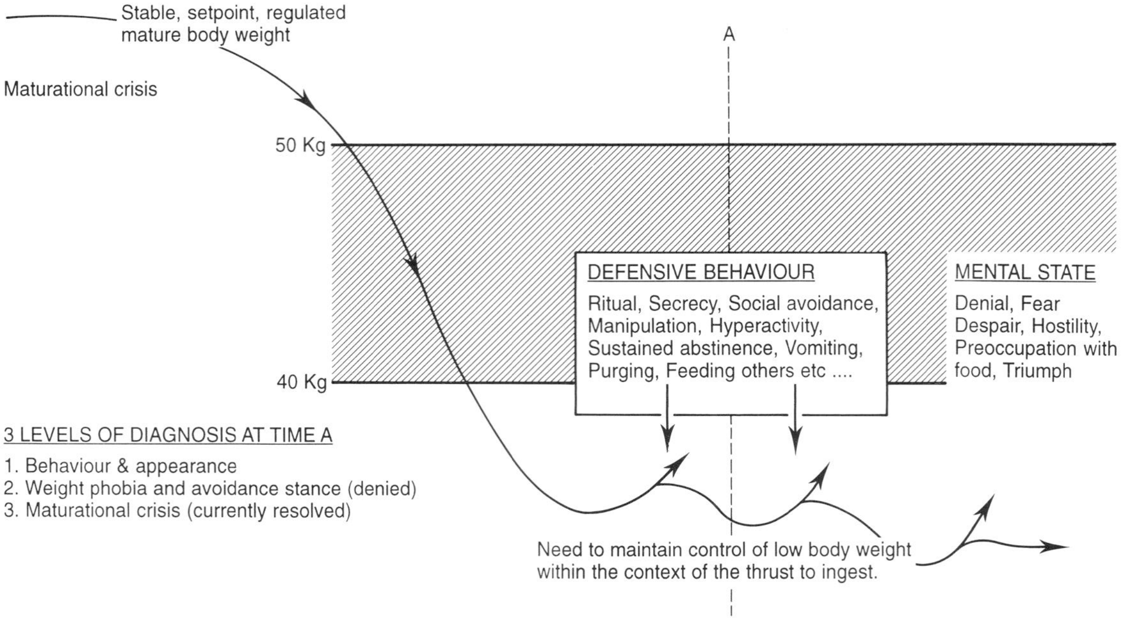

Stable, setpoint, regulated mature body weight

Maturational crisis

A

50 Kg

40 Kg

MENTAL STATE

Denial, Fear Despair, Hostility, Preoccupation with food, Triumph

DEFENSIVE BEHAVIOUR

Ritual, Secrecy, Social avoidance, Manipulation, Hyperactivity, Sustained abstinence, Vomiting, Purging, Feeding others etc .....

Need to maintain control of low body weight within the context of the thrust to ingest.

3 LEVELS OF DIAGNOSIS AT TIME A

1. Behaviour & appearance
2. Weight phobia and avoidance stance (denied)
3. Maturational crisis (currently resolved)

The range of defensive strategies employed to resist the impulse to eat and gain weight include:

- Dietary restriction

- Vomiting if excessive eating has occurred (does the anorectic disappear to the lavatory immediately after a meal?)

- Secret excessive use of laxatives, slimming pills or diuretics

- Excessive exercise

- Vegetarianism

- Protective ritualistic behaviour

- Insistent avoidance of any social contact such as eating with others which may derail the ability to resist eating

- Extreme manipulativeness and temper tantrums, to keep family pressures to eat at bay. Anxious people can be tyrannical as they struggle to minimise their anxieties by controlling social and physical environments. The anorectic's anxiety, focused on the threat of weight gain, is the mainspring of her desperation. Thus the anorectic rapidly comes to be experienced as a tyrant, obstinate and 'very strong willed'.

The strains of sustaining this stance and the isolation and lack of fulfilment that go with it lead sooner or later to exhaustion and despair. On the other hand any failure to protect against even minor weight gain can generate panic and disgust and lead to self-damaging behaviour, e.g. cutting/overdoses. The anorectic is in a no-win situation although she may attempt to represent her state as fulfilling since it is her last refuge and, as already indicated, suicide may be preferable to weight gain. So-called 'depression' may therefore be a prominent feature at any stage but especially so as the disorder becomes chronic.

Level 2:   The phobic avoidance mechanism

Identify the underlying but still conscious psychopathology of the fear of normal body shape and hence normal body weight (weight phobia). This is often denied and may be difficult to elicit until the patient is challenged by attempts to gain weight (as mentioned, a pivotal weight is 7 stones and above). Other defensive manoeuvres may distract from the weight phobia e.g. complaints of abdominal pain or constipation can mask food restriction, vomiting, and alteration in bowel habit due to secret laxative abuse.

Elicit the patient's genuine sense of being fatter than she is. She is as 'fat' as she can afford to be. In her own eyes, her present condition is optimal. The thought of any weight gain will carry with it overwhelming negative meaning which she will express in terms of her 'fatness' and shape. The anorectic perceives herself only in such terms. She may describe body image disturbance in terms of a perceptual distortion e.g 'my stomach/tummy is fat' when she is emaciated, or as a disparagement of a particular area, usually the 'stomach', hips, thighs, bottom or breasts.

Level 3:   The avoided phobic 'object' — the maturational conflict

Try to identify the maturational conflicts that underlie the illness and formulate an hypothesis in experiential, behavioural and social terms. Common themes arise in relation to pubertal development, e.g. sexuality, individuation, autonomy, alienation, ineffectiveness and profoundly low self-esteem.

One problem is that the adolescent developmental conflicts no longer exist in the established 'case'. They have been resolved by the disorder. They may never have been acknowledged. In their place are the new non-specific conflicts that arise in any family if one of its children is wasting away and will not eat despite encouragement. The parents, especially the mother, will feel de-skilled, defeated (for all to see) and helplessly angry. This is what they will want to tell you about. They may well be defensive, expecting to be 'blamed'. It will be important, at the time of the assessment, not only to try and reassure them that they are not 'to blame' but to help them to focus their involvement instead on the time preceding the onset of the anorexia nervosa, when developmental issues will have been critical in relation to the 'patient', and now to re-frame their involvement as one of great importance and responsibility.

Also, formally assess the resources and potential for change in the individual and the family. What psychological resources have this family system and the individuals within it demonstrated in the past in relation to maturational tasks? How enmeshed, conflict avoidant, etc. is it as a family? Sometimes one or other parent will have recognised the onset of the anorexia nervosa early on and then been unable to convince the other parent. More often others e.g. teachers, friends, will have recognised it first.

Remember, do not necessarily be deceived by plausible claims that liberal attitudes or good communication prevail in the family. A major conflict avoidant strategy in such family systems is that of non-communication about salient developmental problems within it.

Look for genetic and physical identifications within the family, role castings within it and also the meaning within it of the existence of the afflicted individual. Why is this child and not another one afflicted? Look at transgenerational family allegiances and alliances both before and since the onset of the illness. For instance, remember that many children are not 'planned', may have turned out to be the 'wrong' gender, may be 'pawns' in a family 'game'. Some (up to 10%) will not have the biological father it is generally believed they have. Examine the dynamics of adoption in a similar way if that has occurred. Such factors may be vital markers of what has gone wrong within the patient's adolescence. Some of the typical challenges that puberty generates and which are the stuff of adolescence and parental reactions are listed in the chart on page 15. Whether parents react supportively and creatively or defensively will depend importantly on what they are being re-exposed to now in relation to their own adolescent adjustments, acknowledged or secret, which may have provided the basis for their marital or other bond.

At this stage it is also useful to search specifically for known prognostic indicators within the individual and the family. Indicators of poor outcome include:

1.   Within the individual —
- duration of illness greater than 10 years
- lowest weight ever within the illness
- poor peer relationships in childhood
- severe bingeing/vomiting behaviour
- severe laxative abuse
- poor impulse control, obsessionality, rigidity
- sexual abuse
- late age of onset
- premorbid obesity
- neurotic/personality disturbance
- high level of denial of illness
- powerful denial of family strains
- past failed treatment

2.   Within the family —
- marital discord
- disturbed family relationships (e.g. extreme dependence on mother, hostility to a distant father)
- parental neurotic character structures
- social class 4/5 background

THE EXPERIENTIAL GULF AND SOME OF ITS ORIGINS

Prepuberty

Puberty

Adolescence

Postpuberty

Asexuality
The family, its mores and social currencies
   traditional
   religious
      masked indifference/ambivalence

Dependent
Compliant
Controlled
Loved
Possessed
Esteemed
Parental values
Parental 'secrets' maintained
Parents' incompatibilities concealed
Family conflict avoided
Parents together
Like father
Like mother
Academically committed

Sexuality (and associated 'fatness')
The outside world, its mores and social currencies
   'progressive'
   nonreligious
      exposed indifference/ambivalence

'Independent'
Rebellious
Impulsive
Rejected
Abandoned
Devalued
Peer values
Parental 'secrets' exposed by re-enactment
Parents' incompatibilities revealed
Family conflict exposed
Parents split
Like mother (and rejected by father)
Like father (and rejected by mother)
Academically indifferent

15

The three levels of diagnosis described above can then allow the formation of a working hypothesis that should be shared with the family as evidence of understanding, inviting 'trust' and potential therapeutic effectiveness, and which will guide initial treatment. One can recognise within each level the DSM-IV / ICD 10 diagnostic criteria (Appendix 1). Height and weight are used to calculate the percentage below mean matched population weight, and compared to standardised tables for age and height (listed at the back of our self-help book, *Anorexia Nervosa: The Wish to Change*). Quetelet's body mass index (BMI) is also used to assess weight loss.

$$BMI = \frac{Weight \ (kg)}{Height^2 \ (m)} \quad \text{— normal adult range is 20-25}$$

Amenorrhoea is an important criterion. If a patient is still menstruating at a low weight is she taking the oral contraceptive pill, or is she vomiting? In patients who vomit and use purgatives the effect of dehydration falsely lowers the weight. Occasionally amenorrhoea can appear before significant weight loss and is related to carbohydrate restriction, but the mechanism is not clearly understood.

The clinical diagnostic process can be supplemented (but not replaced) by the use of standardised instruments for measuring the presence of anorexia nervosa. Commonly used self-report questionnaires include the Eating Attitudes Test [EAT] (Garner et al. 1979) which measures a range of behavioural and symptom parameters in anorexia nervosa, and the Eating Disorder Inventory [EDI] (Garner et al. 1983) which, in addition, assesses the psychological dimension. Both questionnaires can be used as screening instruments and also to assess progress and recovery. The Eating Disorders Examination [EDE] (Cooper et al. 1987) is a semi-structured interview (more of a research tool) which generates a comprehensive description of the specific psychopathology, behavioural and attitudinal features.

PHYSICAL FINDINGS

These are largely related to the biological conservation/withdrawal stance in the face of calorie depletion, to the impact of any bingeing/vomiting/laxative abuse and to other behaviours harnessed by the patient to sustain avoidance of weight gain.

The **General appearance** is one of emaciation. The skin is dry, sometimes with a yellow tinge (carotenaemia), scalp hair is thin and lustreless.

Hypothermia is characteristic and may present with cold intolerance and an inability to compensate for changes in temperature. The hands and feet may be discoloured due to cyanosis and cold with a thready pulse (unless the patient vomits regularly in which case they may be sweating).

Lanugo hair (fine downy hair) can be a feature, particularly on the face, neck, arms, back and legs. (Loss of head hair can be frightening and distressing.)

A callous on the back of the hand may develop from initiating vomiting. Painless hypertrophy of the salivary glands and dental enamel erosion can be features of vomiting. There may be a smell of vomit on the breath. Purpura may result from repeated vomiting or

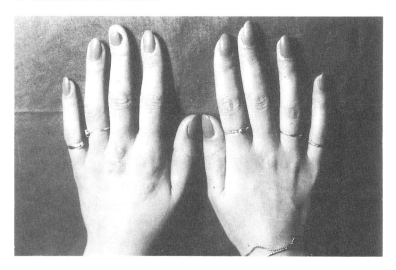

reflect bone marrow aplasia and thrombocytopenia (Sharp and Freeman, 1993). Ankle oedema (particularly in the evening) and periorbital oedema (on waking) reflect laxative abuse. Rebound oedema occurs if purging is stopped abruptly.

Signs of past self-mutilation are not uncommon.

Breast size is reduced (or there is non-development in early onset cases); but there is a normal distribution of secondary sexual characteristics.

The patient is usually full of energy and may wish to stand during the interview. Lethargy is a late feature and may indicate ultimate 'giving up' and/or serious medical complications such as congestive cardiac failure, widespread neuropathy, myopathy and end stage illness.

Thus, abnormalities abound within all the bodily systems.

Gastrointestinal system

Constipation, abdominal bloating and delayed gastric emptying are commonplace. Other complications are also referred to later in the section on vomiting (page 22). Delayed gastric emptying is responsible for the bloated/full feelings that patients report after eating. Uncommonly, gastric dilation and even rupture can occur on refeeding, particularly in young, severely malnourished female patients. Acute pancreatitis has also been reported during refeeding.

Cardiovascular system

Bradycardia is common (less than 60 beats/min and can be as low as 25 beats/min). Blood pressure is low (90/60 mmHg). There may be arrhythmias (palpitations), and a heart murmur (mitral valve prolapse). Peripheral vasoconstriction is a feature. Dehydration and chronic volume depletion can lead to postural hypotension, dizziness and syncope. Rapid pulse and peripheral flushing can follow excessive (secret) bingeing. Cardiac failure may occur during refeeding or as a terminal event.

In association with the above, ECG changes are common, (e.g. low voltage bradycardia, T wave inversion, ST segment depression). It is not possible to predict which patients will develop life threatening symptoms. However, particular cause for concern exists if there are supra-ventricular premature beats, or ventricular tachycardia with or without exercise, (VT can follow emetine use). A prolonged Q-T interval is rare but important as it predisposes to arrhythmias and can cause sudden death.

Renal system

A range of renal abnormalities are commonly found. Decrease in urine concentrating ability and abnormalities in vasopressin secretion may produce a partial diabetes insipidus leading to polyuria. Renal calculi can arise from dehydration. Persistent electrolyte abnormalities resulting from continued vomiting or purgative abuse may lead to permanent renal damage (mesangial hyalinisation and sclerosis and interstitial renal fibrosis). Peripheral oedema is commonly encountered during refeeding, it is usually mild and resolves with a diuresis. A more severe form is found in association with hypoproteinaemia. The resultant fluid shifts can precipitate shock, cardiovascular collapse and renal infarcts. This medical emergency requires intravenous protein replacement among other treatments.

Musculo-skeletal system

Reduction in bone density due to osteoporosis can lead to fractures in the vertebrae, sternum and long bones. Growth is impeded in children. Recent studies show osteoporosis is present within two years of the onset of anorexia nervosa and is correlated with the duration of the illness and BMI (Sharp and Freeman 1993).

Endocrine system

Amenorrhoea can occur prior to major weight loss. There is a complicated relationship between weight, diet and menstruation; the return of menses usually lags behind restoration of normal weight. Bingeing and vomiting at normal weight may account for some cases; it is also diet and 'setpoint' regulated.

Isolated reports have noted that patients gaining weight can conceive prior to the return of menses. Contraceptive advice is often a very important consideration for patients approaching target weight.

Menstruation at apparently low body weight can occur if the patient is vomiting and purging and thereby severely dehydrated. As mentioned earlier the patient continues to menstruate if she is taking the oral contraceptive pill (or depot contraceptive injection).

Symptoms suggestive of hypothyroid disease may present, e.g. cold intolerance, constipation, bradycardia, dry skin, increased relaxation time for deep tendon reflexes. Investigations reveal low/normal thyroxine and thyrotropin. The signs probably reflect a relative deficiency of tri-iodothyronine and these abnormalities return to normal with weight gain. TSH is normal, rT3 is increased. Low T4 and raised TSH suggest pituitary/ hypothalamic origin.

Central nervous system

Within the central nervous system decreased or absent tendon reflexes are an indication of severity, as is muscle weakness and other signs of peripheral neuropathy and myopathy (can the patient stand unaided from a squatting position?). Epileptic fits and tetany can also occur.

Examination of the **respiratory system** and the **abdomen** may reveal complications described in the following sections.

Anorexia nervosa with comorbidity

Comorbidity can compound the medical complications, e.g. young diabetic patients can manipulate their weight at the expense of good diabetic control and increase the risk of complications such as retinopathy and neuropathy (Steel et al. 1987). Meadows and Treasure (1989) report the difficulty of managing Crohn's disease associated with an eating disorder.

In our own service other forms of comorbidity and potential comorbidity have been observed over the last 30 years. Such disorders as cystic fibrosis, hypertrophic cardiomyopathy, the prospect of Huntington's chorea, and similar chronic, possibly genetically determined and ultimately fatal conditions, coming on or worsening in adult life, have been identified and considered to be contributing to the development of the anorexia nervosa. Thus the anorexia nervosa was considered to be protective under such circumstances and most often primed unconsciously by the threat of the other disorder consequent on puberty. Under these circumstances such disorders will, in the first instance, often also have attracted additional meaning for the individuals concerned, which will then have contributed to the anorexia nervosa being the particular response, e.g. identification with a 'bad' aspect e.g. sexual, of the parent who is also the custodian of the genetic defect.

Additional complications resulting from vomiting/laxative abuse

It is very important to identify **any secret background of vomiting and laxative abuse since they increase the severity of the medical complications** through the effect on fluid and electrolyte balance. The recognition of these behaviours may be difficult.

> a.   *Chronic vomiting*

Whereas calorie restriction, based on reduced dietary intake generates a unique kind of starvation (i.e. dietary carbohydrate and fat depletion contrasted with the protein/calorie/essential elements depletion of kwashiorkor), the malnutrition consequent on vomiting and/or major laxative abuse produces a very different clinical picture. Laxative abuse may accompany continued selective dietary carbohydrate and fat restriction or may be associated with frequent vomiting as another defence against indiscriminate binge eating. Thus, if dietary restraint has given way to bingeing with subsequent vomiting as the defence against weight gain, then selective dietary restriction is abandoned and large amounts of carbohydrate and fat may now be consumed indiscriminately. The resulting vomiting and/or laxative abuse can now produce a starvation syndrome more akin to kwashiorkor. In particular, protein deficiency will now also arise.

With severe vomiting (which can be many times per day) major fluid and electrolyte disturbances arise. **Hypokalaemia** and **hypochloraemic alkalosis** occur, blood urea may be elevated due to dehydration and plasma protein levels may be found to be higher than is actually the case.

Vomiting can lead to sore throat, mouth ulcers, erosion of dental enamel, abdominal pain, oesophagitis, haematemesis, and even oesophageal rupture. Emetine poisoning due to use of ipecac may cause irreversible myocardial damage.

b.   *Laxative abuse*

Severe laxative abuse can lead particularly to severe dehydration and electrolyte depletion. Hyponatraemia further compounds the potassium loss as a reduction in the plasma sodium releases rennin angiotensin and aldosterone. Aldosterone then promotes further potassium loss from the kidneys. Laxative abuse can amount to dozens or even hundreds of *Sennacot* or other laxatives being consumed each day. Laxatives are abused because the anorectic feels distended and believes that laxatives will relieve her of the calories she has just consumed. In fact such abuse does not rid her of calories. The initial effect will be to achieve the much needed weight loss but, in the long term, the emerging profound metabolic deficiencies can lead to severe oedema and (to her) terrifying weight gain. Severe laxative abuse results in an alteration in bowel habit, constipation and diarrhoea, rarely steatorrhea, protein losing enteropathy and ultimately malabsorption. Chronic laxative abuse may also lead to the development of an atonic colon because of damage to the myenteric plexus and rectal prolapse which may require surgical correction. Nonspecific inflammation or melanosis can be seen on colonoscopy.

INVESTIGATIONS

Blood tests

Routine investigation should include: Full blood count, electrolytes, chloride, urea and creatinine blood glucose, liver function tests, calcium, phosphate, total protein, albumin, globulins, thyroid function tests (TFT). Consider the need to measure B12, folate, thiamine function, magnesium and zinc levels.

Abnormalities found:

Haematological: Pancytopaenia can occur reflecting bone marrow suppression, neutropenia (granulocyte count of 2000/mm2 requires further investigation). Mild anaemia (normochromic or hypochromic, probably due to subclinical deficiency of iron or folic acid and protein malnutrition). The bone marrow may be hypocellular with the deposition of mucopolysaccharide substances.

Electrolytes: Hypokalaemia is an important complication; it increases the potential for cardiac arrhythmias and the risk of sudden death.

Dehydration results in a disproportionate rise in blood urea compared with creatine.

Liver enzymes can be abnormal (nutritional hepatitis with raised alkaline phosphatase and lactate dehydrogenase). It is important to look for covert alcohol use. Total protein and globulins are often reduced, albumin can be low or normal.

Blood glucose is low, hypoglycaemia is a serious risk factor when weight falls below 33 kg (higher in men). Increased metabolic demands such as those created by infection can then precipitate coma. The Glucose Tolerance Test is abnormal (diabetic type) with a delay in clearing blood glucose and prolonged elevation of plasma insulin which suggest a characteristic degree of insulin resistance.

Serum amylase is often elevated.

Calcium and *phosphate* are often abnormal, hypophosphataemia can lead to serious complications (myocardial/neurological) during refeeding.

Cholesterol and *carotene* levels are elevated.

Thyroid function tests — (see page 21).

ECG rhythm strip

Abnormalities described on page 19. Frequent ECG monitoring is advised in severely underweight patients and those who are vomiting and using laxatives.

Chest X-ray

Chronic respiratory infections, especially tuberculosis, were said to characterise anorexia nervosa in times past. Recently, such cases have been described again. Pulmonary complications can also arise if vomit is inhaled, or if excessive cigarette smoking is a feature of the condition.

Urine analysis

It is a useful adjunct to blood tests to assess renal function by measuring the creatine clearance and as a screen for laxative abuse.

The majority of the above abnormalities are fully reversible if nutritional status is restored to normal, except pathological fractures which can produce chronic pain and deformity. Remineralisation can occur on recovery as seen in women with a past history of anorexia nervosa (Treasure 1987). The role of hormone replacement therapy (HRT) in chronic anorexia nervosa remains uncertain and controversial.

A number of comprehensive reviews of the physical complications associated with eating disorders are available (Bhanji & Mattingly, 1988). A recent article by Sharp & Freeman (1993) highlights the need for an extensive initial physical examination and range of laboratory investigations and electrocardiography. Sharp and Freeman suggest a number of additional investigations including creatinine clearance, bone densitometry.

The majority of the abnormalities noted above resolve with refeeding, but the potential complications of this process suggest the need to continue to monitor and regularly reassess the patient's progress.

PREGNANCY AND MOTHERHOOD IN ANOREXIA NERVOSA

Pregnancy is uncommon but may be achieved through the use of fertility drugs. This is not to be recommended. Labour is often premature. Foetal growth may be impaired. The babies are often small for dates and at birth (Treasure & Russell, 1988) and there is a raised neonatal mortality rate (Brinch et al. 1988). Stunting may result from feeding difficulties during childhood (Van Werzel-Meifler and Wet 1989). Moreover, the existence of anorexia nervosa indicates a degree of immaturity incompatible with the tasks of mothering. Even after recovery from anorexia nervosa any pregnancy is best delayed for some years. It is important to remember that conception can occur during recovery from anorexia nervosa and prior to return of menstruation.

III. TREATMENT

The treatment package which follows is a brief psychotherapeutic intervention with subsequent longer term follow-up with support and reducing amounts of active treatment. It is based on the model of psychopathology described in chapters I and II. A recent treatment study has demonstrated that a brief intervention along these lines (which may be all that can be offered in a local service), can be highly effective for severely ill patients at least during the year following cessation of such treatment (Gowers et al. 1994). However, such brief truncated intervention can be followed by a significant "let down" effect, against which these guidelines attempt to mitigate by recommending further lengthy informed, albeit infrequent, follow-up. Meanwhile we have also shown that a more sustained intervention, still of the kind described here, can substantially reduce long term mortality and is undoubtedly more desirable if possible. For further information about these research findings see Crisp et al. (1991). Our treatment approach is described in more detail elsewhere, and is also the topic of video presentations, including one in which people who have recovered from anorexia nervosa following our treatment discuss their experiences (see Appendix 2).

Personal growth and development is the aim of any such treatment. The developmental flaws and maturational conflicts identified through the assessment need to be addressed. For this to happen the individual will need (through weight gain), to re-engage with normal physical growth involving the reactivation of puberty and the adolescent anxieties which follow. This time, the anorectic and her family will need to be identified experientially with this process. Psychotherapy is required to facilitate this new learning experience and to foster different ways of communicating and problem solving. The 'patient' and the family will have to negotiate the developing separation/individuation processes. For the 'patient' an increasing sense of ownership over the body and impulse control will need to be integrated with an accompanying adequate sense of self and self esteem. Concurrently, the parents may need to begin to move, as much as possible, to new personal and relationship adjustments. Any such shifts, e.g. as the result of improved communication and consequent problem solving, compromise, realignments, would be intended to enable the patient more confidently and securely to grow out of her anorexia nervosa. Without such help the task is that much more difficult.

Growing up cannot be achieved in a matter of months.

Effective treatment, of whatever kind, requires a long term perspective, ideally over 5-6 years. The recommended treatment engagement, in our own specialist centre and given the constraints of our resources, all complemented with specified dietetic advice sessions, is as follows:

Year 1 -	23 psychotherapy sessions	5 dietetic sessions
Year 2 -	12 psychotherapy sessions	3 dietetic sessions
Year 3 -	3 psychotherapy sessions	2 dietetic sessions
Year 4 -	2 psychotherapy sessions	1 dietetic session
Year 5 -	1 psychotherapy session	1 dietetic session
Year 6 -	1 psychotheerapy session	1 dietetic session

Clearly this can only be a guideline and will vary to an extent with each 'case'.

Limited resources affect all psychiatric services. The majority of district services will not have access to this type of specialist treatment intervention yet will encounter patients with anorexia nervosa and be expected to provide treatment.

The following guidelines have been developed in response to numerous requests from practitioners for advice and comprise a briefer but equally valuable intervention plus fewer, but therefore crucially important, sessions subsequently spread over a long period of time.

> *As stated in the preface, this programme is not put forward as ideal but as the absolute minimum of potential professional intervention. It requires sound assessment in the first instance and expert mature psychotherapy thereafter. Thus, the aim of this document has been to give guidance on how to begin to assess and manage anorexia nervosa, at least in the first instance and in a non-specialist setting using basic psychotherapeutic competencies.*

These basic skills (see Appendix 2) include a capacity to work with the transference and interpret it and other aspects of the patient's experience and behaviour as appropriate. It also requires an understanding and control of the countertransference. The treatment focus will usually be the identified maturational conflict preceding the onset of the anorexia nervosa. Sometimes this will need to extend to earlier aspects of the patient's development, e.g. if there has been an important loss to the family system or major abuse, including sexual abuse, at an earlier stage. Anorectics think very concretely, and interpretations especially need to refer back to their weight and shape concerns in terms of the latter's wider meanings, e.g. connections with self-esteem, sexual conflict, right to exist, ownership of the body, physical identification with one or other (bad) parent, parental value judgements and their attitudes to the human body, conditional love, etc. Opportunities frequently exist for timely interpretations of defensive strategies such as denial/avoidance and splitting, often involving transference processes. 'Splitting' of the clinical team and of the team from the parents, with extremes of idealisation and denigration, will require constant reflection and constructive scrutiny by the team. Patients must be protected from experiencing such interventions as persecutory by careful management of countertransference. Thus, experienced supervision of the psychotherapy is most important because of the severity of the psychopathology and the powerful and primitive nature of the psychological defence mechanisms involved in generating and sustaining the condition. Sustaining the supported re-empowerment of the parents within the context of a newly developing family system (e.g. in which the parents become more tolerant of having a mirror held up to themselves and are thereby more able to tolerate their offspring's relatedly expressive adolescence) is ideal.

The treatment package described below provides a framework and a variety of practical tools to help with this task. The details of the treatment programme, i.e. number of sessions, expectations and limitations such as treatment being conditional on weight gain, should be agreed with the patient from the outset and only modified within the context of formal review. (This idea is expanded under Intervention 2 on page 38.)

The Treatment Plan is based on the (self-help) book *THE WISH TO CHANGE* (Crisp et al. 1996) and the *LOG BOOK* (Crisp, 1995) (which are part of this pack).

It begins with the initial assessment which will, hopefully, set the scene for a subsequent initial 12 psychotherapy sessions and related homework by the patient and family.

Ideally, expert advice to the patient from a dietician familiar and comfortable with the present model for the psychopathology and the principles of intervention stemming from it should be available to supplement the programme in the manner described above.

Assessment

As indicated earlier, this is crucial to the whole treatment. The hypotheses that are generated from this meeting direct the subsequent treatment in terms of the focus and style of psychotherapy, e.g. the appropriate balance between the individual and family sessions. The family sessions aim to consolidate progress, to inject new momentum or change. We view the psychopathology as both inherent in the family system and, through biological and introjective processes, also within the 'patient's' mind. For such reasons, and within the brief and condensed intervention described here, the family itself should be involved in a minimum of 3 sessions but up to 8 may be needed.

What are the aims of the intervention?

In the first instance, as described earlier, the parents will, in the normal course of events, need to have come to the assessment, to have engaged systematically in it and to have emerged from it accepting that they too need to adopt the 'patient' roles. Age of patient is no barrier to involving parents. Occasionally it will be appropriate to involve other relatives, a partner or husband as well or instead. This process cannot be sidestepped, especially if the aim is full recovery for the identified patient. As already indicated further details about our assessment process are available. This takes around three hours of face-to-face contact with the individual and the other family members and a further significant period of time of reflection, formulation and documentation including the creation of a weight biography. Sample charts that we use for females and males are reproduced in Appendix 3. Significant milestones including life events can be inserted on the chart which then becomes a valuable *aide-memoire* to treatment. However, weight change during treatment will be best plotted on a larger scale, for example on a sheet of graph paper (see page 34).

It is not appropriate for all patients to aim for a full recovery. For some a safe and stable lower weight may be more appropriate. However, such a weight, e.g. 7 stones, is not compatible with recovery. Whilst it may protect the anorectic from the worst complications of the disorder it will leave her with all the major physical, psychological and social handicaps of chronic anorexia nervosa. These decisions are made with the identified patient herself and also the family at the time of the assessment. They are of course not immutable but will dictate the initial intervention.

The choice to become a 'controlled anorectic' is valid for a number of patients and should not result in a withdrawal of treatment, or 'giving up on the patient'. Acceptance of this decision with the patient is a valuable intervention. The features that guide one in making this decision are chronicity, persistent denial of problems, intractable family difficulties and psychological fragility, as demonstrated by the use of anorexia nervosa as the only successful coping strategy. (See also the list of prognostic indicators on page 14.)

The treatment described in this book can be helpful for these patients. The aims of treatment will however need to be modified. The target weight objective is now the establishment and maintenance of a stable safe low weight without dietary chaos. The social goals are limited to trying to reduce the isolation associated with chronic anorexia nervosa. The psychological work is more concrete and focused on the development of coping strategies rather than exploration and understanding.

The aim of the intervention under these circumstances is to enable the patient to continue to function within the family, in social and work settings, accepting the marked restrictions and limitations imposed by the chronic condition.

Whatever the outcome goal, it is important for the identified patient and the parents to recognise that psychological work needs to be done outside the treatment sessions but influenced by them. If they have not already done so they can be encouraged to read about the disorder on this basis. A book list can be provided (such as those in our self help book and log book). This is a good time to draw the attention of the patient and the rest of the family to organisations such as the Eating Disorders Association here in the UK (or similar relevant organisations in the rest of Europe, North America, etc.)

Identification of target weight

The patient's target weight can now be provisionally identified though not yet shared necessarily with her/him (see page 38). The target weight should be set as being the average weight of the population comparable in height with the patient at the age at which she/he became ill. Such weights can be derived from standard tables for those whose disorders came on at the age of 15 and later (see *The Wish to Change*). It is obviously more difficult to calculate the weights for patients whose anorexia nervosa has arisen within the pubertal process and especially very early on. Target weights for this population need to be derived from growth charts (Tanner and Whitehouse, 1976), using as much information as can be gleaned concerning the premorbid growth and weight characteristics of that individual.

The basic idea behind the selection of the target weight as defined above is that, regardless of the patient's chronological age here and now, academic and career achievements etc. thus far, since the age of onset of the illness her/his psychological development has been arrested (and in fact aborted altogether with the regressive impact of the disorder). In the first instance the task will be to help the patient and her/his family re-engage with the former's developmental challenges at that last stage of previous development. Bearing in mind that these problems previously precipitated the disastrous avoidance response of the anorexia nervosa, the difficulties of the task this time round cannot be over-estimated.

This target weight will be very unlikely to relate precisely to the patient's own premorbid body weight development but is a fair goal which is best presented, when the time comes, as non-negotiable to the patient. Once accepted it can clear the way to concentrating on the psychological tasks in hand. It will only be acceptable within the psychotherapeutic intent outlined in this document. Within it the patient can usually acknowledge and value the justice of having identified the weight in this way. It will require you to understand that the strains confronting her/him are indeed those of, say, the 16-year-old teenager and not, say, the 23-year-old graduate that she has nevertheless become. The more detailed rationale for this aspect of the treatment is elaborated in *Anorexia Nervosa: Let Me Be* (see Appendix 2) and the self-help book (enclosed in the pack). The target weight is ultimately best identified as a horizontal band (target plus 1 kg) on a piece of graph paper on which weight changes can thereafter be plotted as treatment progresses.

THE FOLLOWING LAYS OUT THE IMPORTANT ELEMENTS IN OUR SUGGESTED TREATMENT PLAN. THEY ARE JUST A GUIDE AND SHOULD NOT BE FOLLOWED RIGIDLY. YOUR OWN CLINICAL INTUITION AND JUDGEMENT WILL INFLUENCE THEIR IMPORTANCE AT ANY ONE TIME IN THE SESSIONS.

N.B. These steps are unlikely to work without the pivotal influence of the initial assessment.

The frequency of the sessions will depend in part on the condition of the patient and the practical issue of the resources available.

The face-to-face part of each session is best set at 50 minutes duration and requires the level of psychotherapeutic competence described earlier, incorporating professional relationship and psychotherapy skills. Such skills harness explanation and interpretation appropriately to further understanding and nonjudgemental conduct (control of countertransference), to foster communication. The aim is then to solve identified and re-emerging problems more effectively, building confidence and self-esteem, the ability to tolerate strain including 'adolescent depression', more compromise and consensus in the family, and ultimately enabling personal growth. Some time will need to be set aside after each session for relevant documentation regarding clinical physical status (including body weight), the homework that has been done by the patient and family since the previous session, the essentials of the intervention just concluded and the recording of any significant psychological change evident within these processes. On this basis successive interventions are described below. These are described briefly here and are expanded on and, hopefully, illuminated by the support documents included in the pack and others already mentioned in this book (Appendix 2). As previously indicated, expert supervision of such psychotherapy is an essential adjunct if at all possible. We recognise that this is not always available within multi-disciplinary primary and secondary care systems and lament the fact.

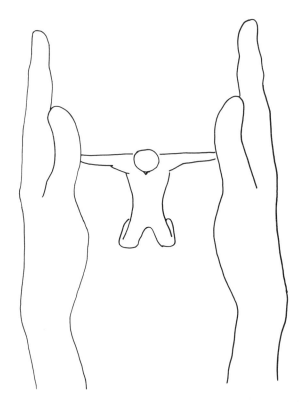

INTERVENTION 1

Assessment interview.

The assessment and consequent engagement in the prospect of change by the patient and family — see pages 31-35. The patient's height and weight should be recorded at the initial assessment. The patient should then be weighed before each subsequent session and the weight plotted on a piece of graph paper (weight record).

INTERVENTIONS 2 -13

The initial intensive psychotherapy.

INTERVENTIONS 2- 5:

FURTHER
ENGAGEMENT
OF THE
PATIENT
(AND FAMILY)

Weekly or fortnightly
sessions.

INTERVENTION 2

Session with patient

1. The need for the patient and her family to formalise their engagement by signing the first page of the log book, which commits them all to treatment, should be discussed. The practical details of doing this should be worked out with the patient.

2. Reconfirm with the patient the expectation that she will consistently gain weight and reach the agreed target weight.

3. Discuss the role of target weight (TW) in treatment and its implications for picking up the threads of adolescent existence at the point at which they had been severed. Where would the patient be now and what would her relationships be with family and peers if the disorder had not supervened. How can things be different this time round. It is important to explain from the beginning of treatment that the patient is choosing to enter into therapy. Accepting treatment involves the decision that

    the patient will give up the weight controlling behaviours and follow the prescribed diet. There is the expectation that the patient will gain weight consistently or hold his/her present weight depending on the formulation and agreed management plan.

    Failure to follow this agreement will lead to discharge from active treatment of the kind being described here and the only alternative will be to see the patient occasionally for support and to troubleshoot physical and psychological crises with voluntary or compulsory admission to secondary care medical and psychiatric facilities when necessary.

4. **Set the target weight (TW)**, draw it as a horizontal band on the graph paper used as the weight record. Anticipate and explore the anxieties relating to the TW and continued weight gain.

    The ability to engage in active therapy being described here will depend very much on the outcome and effectiveness of the important initial assessment.

5. To understand the symptoms and signs and to interpret changes associated with weight gain the clinician requires some understanding of the starvation syndrome (Keys et al. 1950). Of particular concern to the patient is her fear of overeating which is often reinforced when she starts to eat the prescribed diet and feels hungry or craves food. It takes a long time before the patient can rely on her physiology to indicate hunger and satiety. It is vital therefore to give her structure in terms of a prescribed choice-limited eating plan.

    If expert dietary advice is not available, prescribe the weekly diet using diet plan A, B, or C as appropriate (guidance is given in the diet section of the self-help book). The diet will allow the individual to hold their present weight or lead to small predictable weight gain. Give guidelines about the amount of sensible exercise.

Homework for patient:

a) The diet plan should be followed carefully to ensure a consistent and predictable weight change; modifying the diet will lead to unexpected fluctuations in weight and the patient will lose confidence in you. A steady gain of about 1.0 lbs per week (0.5 kg) is the aim. All patients, and in particular those who have been using laxatives or vomiting, and who have now stopped this behaviour, will initially gain weight rapidly. It is important to warn the patient about this and to explain that the weight gain reflects rehydration and/or fluid shifts.

b) Construct a life map (see *The Wish to Change*).

Homework for the family:

Meet briefly with them or write asking them to read the self-help book and the other books recommended in it, in preparation for the family therapy meetings to come.

INTERVENTION 3

Session with patient:

1. Record weight on weight chart. Explore the anxieties and fears related to weight gain.

2. With the patient, draw her weight history on the weight biograph chart (see specimen copy as Appendix 3). Continue to insert age-related life events on it as they emerge as relevant within each session.

3. Explore the benefits and the cost of recovery from anorexia nervosa; the table in the self-help book is a useful guide.

4. Discuss the idea of the life map and make links with the weight biography. Use these tools to continue to identify the developmental and precipitating strains.

Homework for patient:

a) Continue to follow the diet plan.

b) Complete the weight biography, consider additions/changes to the map.

c) Start to construct a family tree.

d) Start to use the diary section of the Log Book. This can then be used as a prompt to relevant issues within the therapy and at the patient's behest. Within the diary the patient can be encouraged to touch on intimate current experience including perception of the therapist but with the knowledge that content is under control.

INTERVENTION 4

Session with patient:

1. Record the current body weight graphically, and look at issues around this.

2. a)   Discuss practical difficulties of sticking to the diet and the feelings associated. Consider practical coping strategies for dealing with the panic associated with eating. Allow the patient to suggest ways he/she can try to relax e.g. listen to music, using art to express feelings, writing, etc. The solutions should not include exercise/activity.

   b)   Remind the patient of the treatment agreement with regard to weight control. The absolute requirement is not to lose weight between sessions and the expectation is to gain steadily in the predictable manner described above. A patient may stop gaining and attempt to hold their weight. The clinician must then decide with the patient whether this reflects ambivalence about recovery or some specific dietary difficulty. If the patient fails to gain weight at the next session then discharge from treatment should be discussed.

   Occasionally 'time out' from the programme can be considered for a patient who loses weight or stabilises at a lower than agreed weight. Time out in this context means stopping regular sessions and giving the patient a period of time of one to three months away from the programme. The aim is to allow the patient to decide about continued weight gain to target weight, or stabilisation at a lower anorectic weight. In the 'time out' period stipulate a reasonable/achievable weight change, i.e. to regain the lost weight but in a longer than normal time scale. Failure to achieve this objective at the end of the 'time out' period should lead to discharge from the programme. The patient should then be reviewed in six months to reconsider treatment options. Emergency medical/psychiatric interventions may be required in between and the patient should be made aware of this possibility.

The exception to this very important rule concerning weight gain is when the patient approaches the 7 stone mark (7 stone in females (44.5 kg) or 8 stone in males (50.8 kg) depending on height). At these weights biological prompts rekindle the pubertal process, the patient experiences a dramatic increase in the intensity of the weight-related panic. This undifferentiated panic can be so intense that the patient stops in her tracks and weight gain ceases. Understanding this signal, anticipating it and using psychotherapeutic competencies is vital to help the patient through this period and forward to ultimate recovery.

At this difficult time a compromise situation may need to be agreed, for example the patient may be allowed to hold her/his current weight for two or three weeks in order to work on these fundamental issues. Any such agreement needs clear boundaries and should not be exploited by the patient as a way to avoid the treatment aim of target weight. If, after the agreed period of stabilisation, the patient is unable to re-engage with weight gain and tackle the weight panic, then the procedures described above should be followed. The patient is invited to review the original treatment plan and its likely alternative, i.e. recovery or chronic anorexia nervosa.

c)   Irrespective of any such major hiccup at this stage, consider again with the patient if she is ready to try to give up the anorexia nervosa.

3.   Look at any additions to

   a)   the life map, and

   b)   the weight biography.

4)   a)   Explore the family tree, look at the family relationships (the 'plot the family' exercise in the self-help book may help as a prompt).

   b)   Plan the first family meeting since the assessment.

Homework for patient:

Start the log book proper, and construct a resource grid from the tables in the log book.

INTERVENTION 5

Session: **FIRST FAMILY MEETING**

Involve a co-therapist of the opposite sex to yourself if possible. Settle the family down comfortably. Notice alignments in their seating preferences; comment non-judgementally. Keep in mind that problems in the family system reflect contributions from everyone. Scapegoating (e.g. that the disorder is due to infidelity by one or other parent) should not be colluded with (e.g. explore why the marriage has proved unfulfilling for that parent). Otherwise begin to look at, for example, likenesses within the family, parents' own adolescences, family relationships — patterns of bonding, role of the identified 'patient' — ways of functioning/ communicating, belief systems. Attitudes to sexuality are clearly fundamental and need to be explored with sensitivity, particularly in those not uncommon cases involving familial or extra-familial sexual abuse.

Homework:

> Send away with some family homework to do before the next family session e.g. Steps 1-15 in the self-help book.

Homework for patient:

> Log book; attempt to write under each of the headings.

INTERVENTIONS 6 - 9

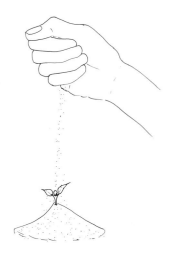

Every two or three weeks

INTERVENTION 6

Session with patient:

1)   Plot weight.

2)   In order to understand the panic feelings associated with weight gain one has to try to focus on the underlying maturational conflicts identified in the original assessment, e.g. sexuality, problems with separation/ individuation, low self-esteem etc. The family session will have highlighted certain areas and the log book can also act as a prompt.

Homework for patient:

Continue to fill in log book.

INTERVENTION 7

Session with patient:

1. Plot weight. Discuss the practical and emotional difficulties resulting from weight gain, use the logbook as a prompt, and keep in mind the formulation with respect to the pubertal conflict.

2. Consider the anxieties associated with the increased time between sessions. This is the first cue to the ending of the intensive treatment. Many patients will have unhappy memories of previous endings. The therapist and the patient need to prepare for it from the beginning of the treatment, particularly in this type of restricted intervention programme. The patient's attitude is likely to be ambivalent. On the one hand there is the potential security of retreating into the avoidant anorectic position again (but with no alternative); on the other hand , if by now there is light at the end of the tunnel for her, she will be panicking and resentful of the prospect of 'abandonment'. Transference issues will abound and must be dealt with. The reality, that there can be sustained understanding and significant contact for some years thereafter can be emphasised but in a way that does not nourish unrealistic hopes of continued dependence.

3. Review cost/ benefit analysis of recovery, the desire, the impact and the ability to change.

Homework for patient:

Continue with the log book review. Draw a second resource grid using the self help book or log book as a guideline.

INTERVENTION 8

Session with patient:

1. Plot the weight.

2. Review the log book and the resource grid.

3. Draw the family relationships, consider any changes. Plan the second family meeting.

Homework for patient:

Continue with the log book.

The treatment programme described in this book is designed to provide a framework for understanding patients with anorexia nervosa and a graded intervention programme for the different stages of recovery.

The focus of the initial work, Interventions 1 - 9, is to make a clear diagnostic formulation. Psychotherapeutic skills are then used to tackle the anxiety associated with the weight phobia and thereby facilitate weight gain to target weight.

Clearly in this type of minimalist package with only 13 principal treatment sessions, many patients will not have reached target weight by Intervention 9. Throughout this book we have struggled with the balance of "ideal management" for patients with anorexia nervosa against the reality of what may be offered in current primary and secondary level services.

If the patient has engaged in treatment and has consistently gained weight in a predictable manner, then this initial phase of treatment can be extended, if it needs to be and if resources are available, to enable the patient to reach the agreed target weight. If, however, any extension of treatment is impossible because of resource constraints and if progress has been limited, then this should be recognised together with the patient, and the psychotherapy should be aimed at containment. Clearly this is not a preferred option because the patient would be at a biologically unstable low weight, with the threat of a further unsupported thrust of growth evoking the danger of a defensive (avoidant) return to low weight status. Another option is to empower the patient to continue to gain weight to TW alone, using the log book as a transitional object. This can only occur if a special psychotherapeutic relationship has been established. Further sessions, contingent on suitable progress, can be offered for a later date.

If, however, progress has been optimal, then there is a shift of emphasis in Interventions 9-13, from weight gain to normal adult body weight maintenance. The psychotherapeutic work now concentrates on the fundamental pubertal conflicts that have been enlivened by weight gain, and the emerging depression through which is the gateway to recovery.

The increased time between sessions is the first indication for the patient of a shift towards greater independence and ultimately the ending of this intensive phase of treatment. Any reduction in therapeutic input will lead the patient to panic, and this needs to be acknowledged and contained, in a way which includes reassurance about long term follow-up. The patient should be encouraged to use the new found skills, personal understanding and coping strategies developed during the initial phases of treatment.

INTERVENTION 9

Session: SECOND FAMILY MEETING

Building on developments (e.g. on the first 15 steps in the self-help book) and foreseeing closure (i.e. next family session may be the last). Again prescribe family homework (e.g. steps 16-30 in the self-help book).

Homework for patient:

a)   Continue with the log book.

b)   Start to consider future plans and try to identify the main emotional problems and the practical issues in relation to food, employment, accommodation.

Dietetic advice is important at this stage (within an extended session if this is not a separate session with a dietician or the team). Ideally, the focus of treatment now may have switched from weight gain to weight maintenance. The diet requires adjustment, and guidance as to how to manage this is available from the dietary advice in the self-help book. Besides actually reducing the diet sufficiently but not too much in order to maintain the target weight, the emphasis needs to shift to recognition of portion size and meal planning, areas which the anorectic patient finds particularly difficult. Many patients also need to learn to budget and shop for food without taking all day. Often the patient will have been reluctant to explain how difficult she finds these basic tasks. Eating in a social context must also be addressed as inability to do this can lead to isolation.

NB. If the patient is at target weight and sexually active there is a risk of conception even though she may not yet have menstruated (see under Intervention 11).

INTERVENTIONS 10 - 13

Every 3-4 weeks.
Preparing for the end of initial phase of intensive psychotherapy.

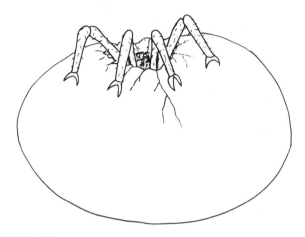

INTERVENTION 10

Session with patient:

1.   Plot the weight.

2.   Continue work on issues raised by weight gain. In particular, if the patient is at target weight, body image and its links with sexuality as a possible signal of impending menarche, are very important areas.

3.   Start thinking with the patient about the ending of the intensive regular session input. This is the first clear signal for the developmental move towards a greater independence.

4.   Review the family situation and any practical issues in relation to food and weight maintenance.

Homework for patient:

Reflect on issues of separation.
Use the log book and redraw the resource grid. Consider again the cost/benefit of recovery and what may prevent weight maintenance.

INTERVENTION 11

Session with patient:

1. Plot weight.

2. Continue to focus on issues surrounding the ending of this stage of the treatment and consider follow-up requirements, bearing in mind the need for long term contact even if infrequent, taking into account what is required but also what is available. The resource grid may be helpful.

3. Review plans for the future. Plan the last family session.

4. Advise, within the context of the therapy, about sexual activity and contraception (see page 26, pregnancy and motherhood section).

Homework for patient:

Use the log book to identify the main hurdles and difficulties in maintaining progress in the future. If it is not to be anorexia nervosa, what alternative strategies can be used in the future.

INTERVENTION 12

Session: FAMILY SESSION

Review of any progress; consolidate changes (e.g. in communication), encourage continuing homework by parents/whole family.

Homework for patient:

> Log book. Focus on saying 'goodbye' so far as the intensive psychotherapy is concerned.

INTERVENTION 13

Session with patient:

1. Plot the weight.

2. Say 'goodbye' satisfactorily. Often this will be a new experience for the patient if previous endings have been equated with rejection. You are helping the patient deal with the end of this phase of active intervention: bear in mind the state of the transference and the fact that the more intensive psychotherapy is now concluded but further contact will be occurring (see below). Make the analogy with natural personal development and the qualitatively changing interaction between parents and children once the latter have developed physically and entered adolescence.

3. Agree long term follow-up, organised and informal, that offers support when required but fosters independence and growth.

4. The expectation is that the individual will continue to hold her weight if at target weight or to continue to gain weight slowly if below target. This is the only 'conditional' aspect of the treatment contract. It needs to be very much separated off from any 'conditional' aspects of positive and negative bonding between the parents and the identified patient. This is a useful vehicle for examining transference issues within the therapy, especially within the context of terminating its active element. Given the maintenance of this one 'condition', normal adolescent turmoil is to be expected, will be 'tolerated' and support given within the promised framework of regular (but increasingly infrequent) contact over the next few years (see page 55).

5. The log book can serve as an *aide-memoire* and important transitional object.

PLANNING FOLLOW UP

Follow up arrangements depend as much on the available resources as on what is required. The patient should be given the security of long-term follow-up. The minimum should be four sessions in the first of the following years, two in the second and third years and one in the fourth and fifth years. The patient needs to know that this structure is in place. These sessions need to be undertaken if at all possible by the person who has done the original psychotherapy and need to relate meaningfully to that work. Throughout this period the patient should be encouraged to continue using her/his log book, especially the diary element within it, and to review progress her/himself in relation to as many of the 30 steps in the self-help book as are seen to be appropriate, and with special attention to any ongoing or developing difficulties for both the patient and the family, in adjusting to the changes taking place.

If your resources permit it the whole family should be included within these follow-up plans; e.g. one, two, or three contacts over the five years.

Against the above background, we recommend that you encourage the patient and family to join the Eating Disorders Association (EDA). This is a lay organisation. It provides an important network of information and support for individuals and their families. It has regional branches throughout the UK. These hold regular group meetings for patients and sometimes also for parents/spouses. An extensive reading list is available from them as well as information leaflets and details of the different specialist services available countrywide. A newsletter and a review journal are also available to subscribers. Patients should be encouraged to try to make contact with their local group if one exists.

The address for the Eating Disorders Association is:

Sackville Place
44 Magdalen Street
Norwich
Norfolk NR3 1JE
Tel: 01603-612414

In other countries there are often similar lay advisory, support and self-help groups. This is especially so in the USA and continental Europe.

When to admit to hospital

The decision is based on psychiatric and physical criteria.

Psychiatric

A full history and mental state assessment should reveal any immediate indications for admission e.g. serious suicidal ideation and intent.

Physical

Weight alone does not necessarily dictate need for in-patient treatment. Other considerations affect the decision such as length of low weight status, rapidity of weight loss, physical complications associated with the weight loss. Symptoms which reflect a dangerously low weight include episodes of hypoglycaemia, a purpuric rash and proximal myopathy.

Welbourne (1992) describes a useful rule of thumb based on weight for making this decision.

Weight as % of Mean Maximum Population Weight (MMPW)	Action
90%	Often considered ideal/ desired weight
85%	Loss of menses
80%	Majority of fashion models
70%	Treat in OPD
65%	Treat in OPD ONLY IF STABLE
60-65%	Consider admission
60%	ADMIT
55%	Consider medical intervention
50%	IMMEDIATE DANGER: Nasogastric tube feed
40%	DEATH

Others have suggested as a rough guide that a BMI of 13.5 or less (i.e. weight 33 kg in a female of average height) is life threatening. As described above there are no absolute guidelines. Associated alcohol abuse, vomiting or purgative use markedly increase the risks of low weight.

Use of the Mental Health Act

It is our belief that anorexia nervosa itself is a state of compulsory detention (Crisp, 1980). Compulsory detention under the Mental Health Act therefore runs the gauntlet of compounding the psychopathology and obstructing the therapeutic relationship. Transference issues become paramount and can, with skill, be surmounted and still turned to advantage. Usually, only patients who chose to accept treatment were admitted to our in-patient unit. The emphasis placed on the assessment can be understood when one is faced with a reluctant and very ill person who is refusing treatment.

The aim of the assessment as described in this book, is to engage the individual, to help them move from rejection to acceptance of the role of a patient. This is usually but not always possible. There may then be occasions where the Mental Health Act is required to treat the patient against her/his will. The situations where this may be necessary include the risk of death through inanition or suicide. Clinicians vary in their understanding of the need to use the Mental Heath Act under these circumstances. Clinical guidelines used by some include comorbidity e.g. depression and suicide risk; or weight criteria e.g. BMI below 14 (higher if vomiting and purging) and/or physical complications.

Physical treatments

Medication

1. Neuroleptics were used frequently in the past as part of treatment. The risk of long term side effects is such that they should only be used in an in-patient setting, if the patient is extremely agitated and needs sedation or if the patient is coincidentally psychotic (very rarely the case).

2. Anti-depressants: some practitioners feel these have a role to play if there is evidence of a depressive illness. Others feel, as we do, that depression is part of the recovery process and that, usually, it should be treated with psychotherapy.

    Anti-depressants can have an adverse effect in that they can lead to weight gain, or as with the new selective serotonin re-uptake inhibitors can interfere with appetite regulation, and thereby increase the patient's feeling of loss of control.

3. Benzodiazepines: some authors consider anorexia nervosa to be a form of addictive behaviour in which drugs with an addictive potential are contra-indicated.

Laxative prescription

Patients who are restricting their food intake will often suffer from constipation. The most appropriate treatment is food but it may be that the patient complains of persistent constipation. This presents a dilemma — i.e. should laxatives be prescribed? If the constipation does not respond to dietary manipulation a cautious and time-limited prescription of laxatives may be used and the risk of abuse considered.

ECT is rarely indicated. The severe depression that can arise within anorexia nervosa hardly ever responds to it. The impaired sleep characteristic of anorexia nervosa (early morning waking) is a function of the malnutrition. Psychosurgery is virtually never indicated.

IV. TERTIARY REFERRAL

Relationship to specialist centres

The number of specialist centres is increasing but this spread is still patchy. The services that you might hope for from such centres would include:

* an assessment service;

* an in-patient treatment unit with a long-term follow-up programme for patients who remain within the treatment agreement;

* an out-patient treatment service;
  this includes individual and family psychotherapy with dietetic support. In the recent past we have run an out-patient treatment group package; this requires caution and careful selection of patients, and constant attention to the risk of competitive weight loss. Group treatment should be offered to parents concurrent with the patient group.

* a liaison and telephone advice service;

* a peripatetic service capable of providing advice locally, e.g. a one-off assessment and guidance about treatment if the patient is acutely ill but no beds are available centrally.

Indications for referral

* Failed out-patient/in-patient treatment locally.

* An expert opinion of a case to guide further treatment locally.

• A second opinion.

• The best place to admit a severely physically ill anorectic is a specialist eating disorder service within which reside the skills, hopefully, to enable the anorectic to start eating normally. Even the most acutely and terminally ill anorectic is, in principle, best helped in this way. Unfortunately such services are rare and seriously over-subscribed. Medical attempts to help the terminally ill anorectic to survive may simply comprise the need to get nourishment into the patient. If this situation arises then we recommend nasogastric feeding thereby using the gut; major difficulties can arise using intravenous feeding.

POSTSCRIPT

Finally, although sometimes difficult to accept, it cannot be overstated that anorexia nervosa is a crippling and not infrequently fatal condition, probably the most severely so within the mental health field. It is not a 'frivolous' or trivial one as is sometimes portrayed. Afflicted individuals cannot always be helped to recover; others will fail to survive despite our and your best efforts. We have written this book in an endeavour to enhance such efforts.

In the absence of recovery, anorectics can often be helped to adapt and survive through to old age. Under these circumstances health care costs can be very high if support is not highly professional. We recommend that such support is based on the principles outlined in this book moderated by the more modest goal of survival (see page 32). Guidelines for this also exist in our self-help book.

★　★　★　★

REFERENCES

BHANJI S & MATTINGLY D (1988) *Medical Aspects of Anorexia Nervosa.* Wright, London.

BRINCH M, ISAGER T, & TOLSTRUP K (1988) Anorexia nervosa and motherhood: reproductional pattern and mothering behaviour of 50 women. *Acta Psychiatrica Scandinavica* **77** 90-104.

BRÜCH H (1978) *The Golden Cage.* Open Books, New York.

COOPER Z & FAIRBURN C (1987) The Eating Disorder Examination: a semi-structured interview for the specific psychopathology of eating disorders. *International Journal of Eating Disorders* **6** 1-8.

CRISP A H (1967) Anorexia nervosa. *Hospital Medicine* (May) 713-718.

CRISP A H (1977) The differential diagnosis of anorexia nervosa. *Proceedings of the Royal Society of Medicine* **70** 686-694.

CRISP A H (1980) *Anorexia Nervosa: Let Me Be.* Ballière Tindall, London. Reprinted 1995 by Lawrence Erlbaum Associates.

CRISP A H (1995) *Anorexia Nervosa: Patient Log Book.* Lawrence Erlbaum Associates, Hove.

CRISP A H (1995) Anorexia nervosa in a young male. In: Werne J (Ed) *Treating Eating Disorders.* Jossey Bass, San Francisco.

CRISP A H (1996) Anorexia nervosa: A dyslipophobic flight from growth. In: Garner D M & Garfinkel P E (Eds) *Handbook of Treatment for Eating Disorders.* Guilford Press, New York.

CRISP A H, CALLENDER J S, HALEK C & HSU L K G (1992) Long-term mortality in anorexia nervosa. A 20-year follow-up of the St George's and Aberdeen cohorts. *British Journal of Psychiatry* **161** 104-107.

CRISP A H, JOUGHIN N, HALEK C & BOWYER C (1996) *Anorexia Nervosa: The Wish to Change.* 2nd Edition. Psychology Press, Hove.

CRISP A H, NORTON K, GOWERS S, HALEK C, BOWYER C, YELDHAM D, LEVETT G & BHAT A (1991) A controlled study of the effect of therapies aimed at adolescent and family psychopathology in anorexia nervosa. *British Journal of Psychiatry* **159** 325-333.

GARNER D M & GARFINKEL P E (1979) The Eating Attitudes Test: an index of symptoms of anorexia nervosa. *Psychological Medicine* **9** 273-279.

GARNER D M, OLMSTED M P & POLIVY J (1983) Development and validation of a multidimensional eating disorder inventory for anorexia nervosa and bulimia. *International Journal of Eating Disorders* **2** 15-34.

GOWERS S G, NORTON K R W, HALEK C & CRISP A H (1994) Outcome of out-patient psychotherapy in a random allocation treatment study of anorexia nervosa. *International Journal of Eating Disorders* **15** 165-177.

KEYS A, BROZEK J, HENSCHEL A, MICHELSON O & TAYLOR H L (1950) *The Biology of Human Starvation*. University of Minnesota Press, Minneapolis.

MEADOWS G & TREASURE J (1989) Bulimia nervosa and Crohn's disease: two case reports. *Acta Psychiatrica Scandinavica* **79** 413-414.

MINUCHIN S, ROSMAN B L & HARDING B (1978) *Psychosomatic Families: Anorexia Nervosa in Context*. Harvard University Press, Cambridge, Mass.

RATNASURYA R H, EISLER J, SZMUKLER G J & RUSSELL G F M (1991) Anorexia nervosa: outcome and prognostic factors after 20 years. *British Journal of Psychiatry* **158** 495-503.

SHARP C W and FREEMAN C P L (1993) The medical complications of anorexia nervosa. *British Journal of Psychiatry* **162** 452-463.

STEEL J M, YOUNG R J, WYOD G G & MacINTYRE C C A (1987) Clinically apparent eating disorders in young diabetic women: associations with painful neuropathy and other complications. *British Medical Journal* **297** 859-862.

TANNER J M & WHITEHOUSE R H (1976) Clinical longitudinal standards for height, weight, height velocity, weight velocity, and stages of puberty. *Archives of Disease in Childhood* **51** 170-179.

THEANDER S (1985) Outcome and prognosis in anorexia nervosa and bulimia: some results of previous investigations compared with those of a Swedish long term study. *Journal of Psychiatric Research* **19** 493-508.

TREASURE J L, FOGELMAN I, RUSSELL G F M & MURBY B (1987) Reversible bone loss in anorexia nervosa. *British Medical Journal* **295** 474-475.

TREASURE J & RUSSELL G F M (1988) Intrauterine growth and neonatal weight gain in anorexia nervosa. *British Medical Journal* **296** 1038.

Van WERZEL-MEIFLER G & WET J M (1989) The offspring of mothers with anorexia nervosa: a high risk group for undernutrition and stunting. *European Journal of Paediatrics* **149** 130-135.

WELBOURNE J (1992) Slide presented at the Eating Disorder Conference, Institute of Psychiatry, London.

APPENDIX 1

DSM-IV AND ICD 10 CRITERIA FOR THE DIAGNOSIS OF ANOREXIA NERVOSA

DSM-IV
Diagnostic criteria for 307.1 Anorexia Nervosa

A. Refusal to maintain body weight at or above minimally normal weight for age and height, (e.g. weight loss leading to maintenance of body weight less than 85% of that expected; or failure to make expected weight gain during period of growth, leading to body weight less than 85% of that expected).

B. Intense fear of gaining weight or becoming fat, even though underweight.

C. Disturbance in the way in which one's body weight or shape is experienced, undue influence of body weight or shape on self evaluation or denial of the seriousness of the current low body weight.

D. In postmenarchal females, amenorrhea, i.e., the absence of at least three consecutive menstrual cycles. (A woman is considered to have amenorrhoea if her periods occur only following hormone, e.g. oestrogen, administration.)

ICD 10
F50 - F59 Behavioural syndromes

Diagnostic guidelines

For a definite diagnosis, all the following are required:

(a) Body weight is maintained at least 15% below that expected (either lost or never achieved), or Quetelet's body-mass index[1] is 17.5 or less. Prepubertal patients may show failure to make the expected weight gain during the period of growth.

(b) The weight loss is self-induced by avoidance of "fattening foods". One or more of the following may also be present: self-induced vomiting; self-induced purging; excessive exercise; use of appetite suppressants and/or diuretics.

(c) There is body-image distortion in the form of a specific psychopathology whereby a dread of fatness persists as an intrusive, overvalued idea and the patient imposes a low weight threshold on himself or herself.

(d) A widespread endocrine disorder involving the hypothalamic — pituitary — gonadal axis is manifest in women as amenorrhoea and in men as a loss of sexual interest and potency. (An apparent exception is the

---

[1]Quetelet's body mass index = $\dfrac{\text{weight (kg)}}{\text{height (m)}^2}$ to be used for age 16 or above.

persistence of vaginal bleeds in anorexic women who are receiving replacement hormonal therapy, most commonly taken as a contraceptive pill.) There may also be elevated levels of growth hormone, raised levels of cortisol, changes in the peripheral metabolism of the thyroid hormone, and abnormalities of insulin secretion.

(e) If onset is prepubertal, the sequence of pubertal events is delayed or even arrested (growth ceases; in girls the breasts do not develop and there is a primary amenorrhoea; in boys the genitals remain juvenile). With recovery, puberty is often completed normally, but the menarche is late.

Differential diagnosis

There may be associated depressive or obsessional symptoms, as well as features of a personality disorder, which may make differentiation difficult and/or require the use of more than one diagnostic code. Somatic causes of weight loss in young patients that must be distinguished include chronic debilitating diseases, brain tumours, and intestinal disorders such as Crohn's disease or a malabsorption syndrome.

APPENDIX 2

SUPPORTING INFORMATION

Included in this pack are the *Patient's Log Book* and the self-help book, *Anorexia Nervosa: The Wish to Change*. The following information about some other documents and videotapes which we have produced may also be helpful.

Anorexia Nervosa: Let me be is now published by Lawrence Erlbaum Associates and can be obtained by mail order. (It is also available in public libraries.)

Video tapes:

> Anorexia Nervosa: Assessment of the Psychopathology
>> A 2-hour teaching tape on the assessment of one case, originally videoed and edited for the Thames TV programme 'The Treatment'.

> Anorexia Nervosa: Diagnostic issues, physical complications, prevalence, models of psychopathology; *and*

> In-patient and out-patient treatment of Anorexia Nervosa.
>> Lectures recorded at the 1992 St George's Eating Disorders conference.

> Recovery from Anorexia Nervosa: Professor Crisp talks with ex-sufferers.

These videotapes can all be purchased from Mrs H Humphrey (Assistant to Professor Crisp) at the following address:

> Psychiatric Research Unit
> Atkinson Morley's Hospital
> Copse Hill, London SW20 0NE.

CRISP A H (1996) Anorexia nervosa: A dyslipophobic flight from growth. In: Garner D M & Garfinkel P E (Eds) *Handbook of Treatment for Eating Disorders.* Guilford Press, New York.

> This chapter deals with the psychotherapeutic issues in more detail than the present book allows.

APPENDIX 3: St George's Eating Disorders Weight Biography (Females)

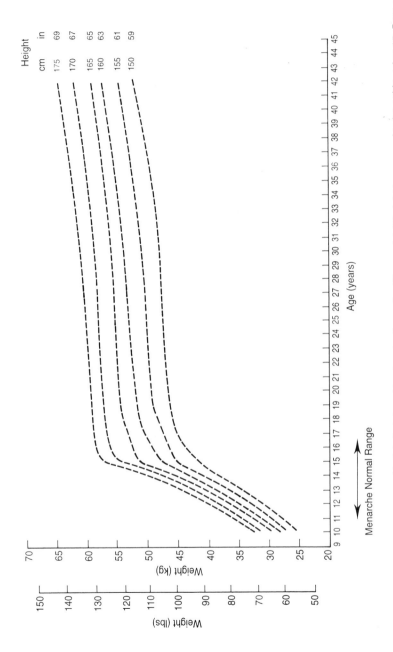

Standards are of mean weight at each age and height but do not imply rate of growth with age. Adult height is assumed to be achieved at 15. Data at this age in these graphs are taken from figures in Kemsley (1953/4) Ann. Eugen. London, 16, p 316 - 334. Below this age weights are calculated from this data in terms of mean percentages of adult weight achieved at different ages as derived from figures in Scott (1955) London County Council Survey.

APPENDIX 4: St George's Eating Disorders Weight Biography (Males)

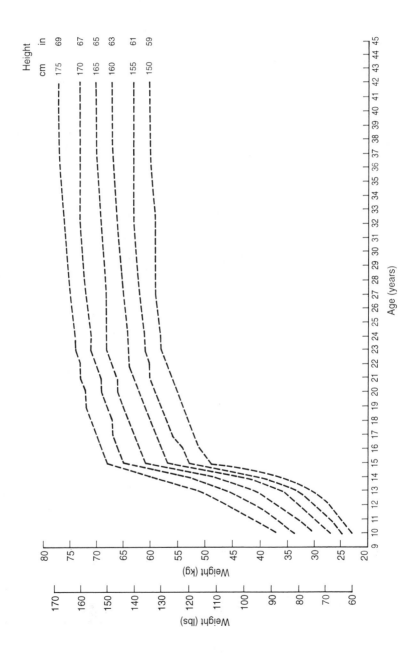

DISCOUNT ORDER FORM

10 copies or more 20%

20 copies or more 25%

30 copies or more 30%

We are pleased to be able to offer discounts on multiple-copy orders of the following books by Professor Arthur Crisp

Anorexia Nervosa: The St. George's Approach To Assessment And Treatment (Clinician's Pack)
☐ 0-86377-412-1 1995 £25.00 $40.00
(3 volume set - includes Anorexia Nervosa: St. George's Approach, Anorexia Nervosa: And The Wish to Change, Anorexia Nervosa: Patient's Log Book)

Anorexia Nervosa: And The Wish To Change
☐ 0-86377-408-3 1996 £9.95 $15.95 pbk

Anorexia Nervosa: Patient's Log Book
☐ 0-86377-407-5 1995 128pp. £9.95 $15.95 pbk

Anorexia Nervosa: Let Me Be
☐ 0-86377-383-4 1995 208pp. £9.95 $15.95 pbk
(first published 1980)

Name and Delivery Address (capitals please)_____

_____

_____

☐ **I enclose a cheque for £**_____ *(Cheques should be drawn on a U.K. bank, and should be made payable to Direct Distribution. Eurocheques must be in £ Sterling only.)*

☐ **I authorise you to debit my credit card with the amount of £** _____

My Access/American Express/Mastercard/Visa No. is: _____

Expiry Date_____Date _____Signature _____

Name (capitals please)_____

Credit Card Address (if different from above) _____

_____

_____

☐ **Please invoice me**

POSTAGE AND PACKING: Books are sent post free within the UK if the order value is over £20.00/$30.00. Otherwise add £2.00/$3.00. European orders over £30.00/$45.00 are also sent post free. Otherwise add £3.00/$4.50. Outside Europe please add 15% of the total value of your order.

PLEASE PHOTOCOPY AND FAX OR MAIL TO:

PSYCHOLOGY PRESS
Direct Distribution, c/o Afterhurst, 27 Church Road, Hove,
East Sussex, BN3 2FA United Kingdom
Tel: (01273) 748 427 Fax: (01273) 205 612
email: dirdist@erlbaum.co.uk